Bible Verses on Prayer

Prayers for Healing and Prayers for Strength

Carol Lee

Copyright © 2015 Carol Lee

All rights reserved. This book or any portion thereof may not be reproduced or used in any manner whatsoever without the express written permission of the publisher except for the use of brief quotations in a book review.

Printed in the United States of America

First Printing, 2015

ISBN-10: 1519135505
ISBN-13: 978-1519135506

CONTENTS

1 Jesus the Healer   5

2 Prayers for Healing   11

3 Prayers for Strength   17

4 How to Pray for the Sick   27

1

JESUS THE HEALER

Jesus is your healer. Right now, close your eyes and declare that you are my healer. You are my present healer. You are my great physician now. It is God's will that you walk in divine healing. The scripture says Jesus healed all that were sick. Jesus heals completely. His work is perfect. In Matthew 4: 23 says, "And Jesus went about all Galilee, teaching in their synagogues, preaching the gospel of the kingdom, and healing all kinds of sickness and all kinds of diseases among the people. Then his fame went throughout all Syria; and they brought to Him all sick people who were afflicted with various diseases and torments, and those who were demon-possessed, epileptics, and paralytics; and He healed them."

These were all manner of sickness and diseases. Whatever sickness or diseases, Jesus healed them all. Philippians 2:9 says, " Therefore God also has highly exalted Him and given Him the name which is above every name, that at the name of Jesus every knee should bow, of those in heaven, and of those on earth, and of those under the earth, and that every tongue should confess that Jesus Christ is Lord, to the Glory of God the Father.

Every disease and sickness has a name. As long as it has the name, it has to bow to the Lordship of Christ. The name of Jesus has the highest authority. Sickness and disease has no authority over your life. It has no legal right to dwell in your body. Therefore it must be ejected with immediate effect.

There was a man down in the valley, a leper that would not dare to climb up the mountain. If he had gone to the service, he would have been stoned because of his leprosy. So, he goes and waits for the master down in the valley. Matthew 8 says, when Jesus came down from the mountain – there came a leper; saying, "Master, if it's your will, you will make me whole." Jesus spoke that eternal word that is still echoing throughout history – I will make you whole. Instantly that man was healed. The leprosy disappeared instantly.

He had just healed the multitudes earlier and here we find an individual that did not even attend the service, but yet Jesus responds to him. In the same chapter when Jesus was on his way to Simon Peter's house, a centurion approaches Jesus and he says, "Lord, Lord…my servant is laying sick." Jesus without hesitation says, I'll come and healed him. The Son of God had every right to say, I am tired. Come back tomorrow. I've just ministered to the thousands this morning and thousands were healed. Why didn't you come and be there?

Instead Jesus says, I'll come and heal him. The centurion says, I am not worthy that you should come into my house. Just say the word and my servant will be healed.

As Jesus gets to Simon Peter's house, his mother in-law is lying there with fever. Jesus stood over her. His shadow covered her and the moment His shadow covered her, sickness died!

For in the presence of Jesus, sickness cannot live. Sickness always dies in the presence of the Lord. Whatever your problem is, should it be cancer or any kind of disease – it has to die in the presence of the

Lord. In the presence of the Lord, cancer dies. Matthew 8:16-17 says, "When evening had come, they brought to Him many who were demon-possessed. And He cast out the spirits with a word, and healed all who were sick, that it might be fulfilled which was spoken by Isaiah the prophet, saying: "He Himself took our infirmities and bore our sickness." In the same chapter of Matthew, a man who is demon-possessed is on the other side of the lake. All of a sudden; Jesus says, "Let's go to the other side." Jesus commands that they go into a boat to the other side of the lake.

Why did Jesus go to this man?

No matter where you are, Jesus is able to reach out to you and heal you. You do not need to be in any prayer meeting. Right on that bed in the hospital, Jesus is able to reach out to you and touch you. The power of God is present to heal.

2

PRAYERS FOR HEALING

Bind, in Jesus' Name every sickness or disease that the enemy wants to use to stop your destiny. Refuse every genetic diseases that has ruled your family for generations past, in the Name of the Lord. Pray for grace to walk in obedience so the diseases of the Egyptians will not come upon you. Take authority over the root of cancer, and command its negative cells to die. Plead the blood of Jesus against every form of torment, whether physical or spiritual. Take authority over binding diseases, such as arthritis, and command that their hold be broken.

Cancel the bondage of genetic diseases in your family back to ten generations.

Pray that the anointing of God will flow from your life to bring healing, deliverance and hope to others.

Pray to release yourself by faith from every disease that may have come upon you through unforgiveness.

Begin to thank God for his covenant Name of Jehovah Rapha.

As you lay your hand on the area of your affliction, remind the Lord of his covenant to heal.

Speak to everything that seems to be a mountain relevant to your health and command it to move, in the Name of Jesus.

Proclaim that the mountain of sickness you see today, you will see no more.

Command every disease in the bones to die, in the Name of Jesus.

Stand on His Word that says He heals all diseases, and confess that all the diseases in your body are healed.

Take authority over every disease of the heart, and receive your healing.

Speak the Word of God to each virus and command it to die, in the Name of Jesus.

Take authority over strokes and blood problems, and receive your healing.

Take a step of faith and, and declare your healing before it is manifest physically.

Hand over the ailment, which experts said could not be healed, and receive your healing.

Confess by faith that your healing will spring forth.

Give God praise, and confess that you are coming out of the bed of illness.

With your mouth, pronounce healing, deliverance and salvation.

Above all, begin to worship God for who He is. Lift Him up above your circumstance. Lift Him up above your immediate situation. As you worship Him, He is magnified in your life. No sickness and disease can stand in the power of worship. Worship expels the anointing of darkness.

When you begin to worship God, His presence is released. And as his presence released, it comes with His power. The power of God breaks and destroys every yoke. It breaks and destroys the yoke of sickness. The power of God breaks and destroys every bondage.

Right now, begin to lift up your voice and worship Him. Let the anointing of God be released over your life. As you worship in spirit and in truth, you will begin to experience his presence and his power – that's when the anointing of healing will be released over your life.

Press in and take your eyes off from your infirmity. Focus on His healing power and ability.

He is the healer. He is the same, yesterday today and forever.

Healing Verses:

Isaiah 58:8

Matthew 4:23

Matthew 9:35

Luke 6:19

Luke 9:6

Luke 9:11

Luke 13:32

John 5:1

John 6:2

John 7:23

John 9:13

Acts 10:38

Revelation 22:2

3

PRAYERS FOR STRENGTH

Thank the Lord, who is your strength. Give God praise, because He causes you to triumph at all times. Thank the Lord, because before the battle began He declared you a conqueror. Thank God, because the battles that you see today you shall see no more. Bless the Name of the Lord, because He makes a way for you in the wilderness and causes streams to flow in the desert places.

Pray to receive God's anointing for courage and strength to face the battles of life.

Declare that in spite of what you are going through, you will possess your possession.

Declare that in spite of what you are going through, you will inherit what God has earmarked for you.

Pray that God will send encouragers to you to lift you up in your low moments.

Pray to receive courage to take up your position until you win.

Pray for wisdom to always draw strength from the Lord for all situations.

Pray for the grace to look above the challenges you are experiencing and to see the victory ahead.

Pray that as you wait upon the Lord you will receive His anointing for victory.

Thank God for giving you a heart that is able to overcome.

Declare by faith that no matter what you go through, your hope will be in the Lord.

Pray to receive God's answer for every troubling situation you are going through.

Declare by faith that you will continue to wait until your change comes.

Declare that in His Word He promised not to bring you to shame.

Declare that in His Word He promised never to leave nor forsake you.

Pray to receive the peace of God that surpasses all understanding.

In the face of battle, declare that with God all things shall be possible.

Thank the Lord, because He will give you the faith that will see you through what you are going through.

Verses for Strength:

Isaiah 40:29

Exodus 15:2

Deuteronomy 11:8

1 Samuel 2:9

1 Samuel 2:10

1 Samuel 30:6

2 Samuel 22:33

2 Samuel 22:40

1 Chronicles 16:11

1 Chronicles 16:27

1 Chronicles 29:12

2 Chronicles 16:9

Nehemiah 6:9

Nehemiah 8:10

Job 4:3

Job 4:4

Psalm 18:32

Psalm 18:39

Psalm 22:19

Psalm 28:7

Psalm 28:8

Psalm 29:11

Psalm 33:16

Psalm 33:17

Psalm 46:1

Psalm 59:9

Psalm 59:17

Psalm 68:35

Psalm 73:26

Psalm 84:5

Psalm 86:16

Psalm 89:17

Psalm 89:21

Psalm 96:6

Psalm 105:4

Psalm 118:14

Psalm 119:28

Isaiah 12:2

Isaiah 28:6

Isaiah 33:2

Isaiah 35:3

Isaiah 40:29

Isaiah 40:31

Isaiah 41:10

Isaiah 45:5

Isaiah 45:24

Isaiah 49:5

Isaiah 58:11

Jeremiah 16:19

Daniel 10:18

Daniel 10:19

Habakkuk 3:19

Zechariah 10:12

Luke 22:43

Romans 4:20

Ephesians 3:16

Philippians 4:13

Colossians 1:11

Colossians 2:7

2 Thessalonians 3:3

2 Timothy 4:17

Hebrews 11:34

Revelation 3:8

CAROL LEE

4

HOW TO PRAY FOR THE SICK

Much uncertainty exist when praying for the sick people. How do we go about? Is it the Lord's will that the person should be healed? Do all illnesses come from the devil? May only someone with the gift of healing pray for the sick? The following are basic guidelines that you can use whenever someone is ill.

1. Illness can basically have three causes:

    a) It can be because of sin in your life,

b) It can be a demonic attack and

c) Normal sickness that the Lord allows in your life.

2. When you are ill, the first basic question you can ask yourself is: Is there any conscious unconfessed sin in my life? If so, ask the Holy Spirit to reveal it to you. Confess it before the Lord and accept His forgiveness. If the Lord leads you, you can pray with a fellow believer about the matter and bring it into the light with him or her. It often happens that a person is healed as soon as they have confessed their sin. James 5:16 – "Therefore confess your sins to each other and pray for each other so that you may be healed." 1 Corinthians 11:27-32 says illness can be caused by the improper use of communion: "Therefore, whoever eats the bread or drinks the cup of the Lord in an unworthy manner will be guilty of

sinning against the body and blood of the Lord. A man ought to examine himself before he eats of the bread and drinks of the cup. For anyone who eats and drinks without recognizing the body of the Lord eats and drinks judgment on himself. That is why many among you are weak and sick, and a number of you have fallen asleep. But if we judged ourselves, we would not come under judgment. When we are judged by the lord, we are disciplined so that we will not be condemned with the world." This "unworthy manner" is often indicative of an unconfessed sin in a person's life. When you pray for the healing of someone else, ask the Holy Spirit to show the person any form of sin in his life that has not yet been confessed and that he will be willing to confess it and turn from it.

3. Illness that comes from the evil one must be resisted in Jesus' Name. The problem is knowing when it is an attack from the evil one. Pray to the Lord for discernment. He is faithful; He will show you what the situation is. In a case where you are not certain at all, pray anyway and say "Satan, I refuse to accept any form of illness that comes from you, I refuse it in the Name of Jesus and I resist any form of pain or illness which you bring over me. In the Name of Jesus, I resist you and your attacks and command you to withdraw yourself from me. Satan can also cause illness in a person's life if there is occultic bondage in his life. If black magic is practiced on him or by means of curses that have been spoken against him. In such cases the person must be delivered from this bondage and the curses must be broken in the Name of Jesus. Black magic only works when

someone is not saved or if there is unconfessed sin in a person's life.

4. Many people think that if we go to the doctor and receive medicine, God is not involved in the healing. It is definitely wrong to think so. God was and is involved in the development of medical science and he uses doctors and medication to heal people. Therefore it is important to pray for the doctor when you go for an appointment; that he will make the correct diagnosis and prescribe the right medication.

5. The Lord may have a specific reason if he allows sickness in your life. Ask the Lord to reveal the reason. Accept the fact that God is not obliged to to answer, and that He may choose to keep silent. In cases like these it is best to accept God's plan and to be still before the Lord.

6. People sometimes think there is something wrong with them when they are ill, that they do not have enough faith to be healed. It is true that God expects faith from us. But God heals regardless of our faith.

7. Sometimes people do not want to be healed because they enjoy the attention and sympathy, or they don't want to go back to work to take up their responsibilities again. Pray for a willingness to recover and receive healing.

8. Pray for wisdom when you pray for someone's healing. Pray for the guidance of the Holy Spirit. Someone may have heart problems for instance, and we know that God can heal that. However, if the person is overweight and eats too much, it would be more fitting to pray for self-control, so that he can discipline himself by eating less and losing weight. That will take away the cause of the

problem. Ask the Lord what causes the illness. It can be unconfessed sin from the past; because of occultic bondage; the Lord sometimes allows it to teach the person something, or it can simply be an attack from the evil one. Depending on the situation, we should pray for the person in a different way every time. The Lord can allow sickness in a person's life to purify him; the fruit thereof is sanctification.

9. Enrich your prayers with scripture when you pray for the sick. Pray according to the promises of God. Also, remember that not all promises are relevant or valid in every case.

10. Remember to saturate your prayer with praise and worship when praying for a sick person. It gives glory to God's work and faith to your own heart. The weapon of praise and worship is

especially important in the case of a demonic onslaught.

11. The principles of spiritual warfare, our authority in Christ and His victory over the evil one, are of utmost importance when there is the possibility of a demonic onslaught. We must bind the evil one in the Name of Jesus, break and resist his works.

12. Testify to what the Lord has done. It gives others confidence to pray and it strengthens their faith in God's ability to heal. Testimonies like these often contribute to the conversion of others and the returning of those who have backslidden.

13. Make a note when you pray for someone who is ill and write down the answers. You will be astonished when you see how many people that you have prayed for, were healed.

14. The father, being the head and priest of the home should pray for his family if someone is ill.

However, the whole family must learn to pray together for a sick member of the family. When a family prays together, it strengthens family ties and sympathy for each other. We are inclined not to pray if we visit a doctor. This is wrong.

15. According to research about 50-80% of patients that visit doctors are people suffering from psychosomatic diseases. It means that these illnesses originate from psychological or spiritual problems. There is often bitterness, hatred, unforgiveness, stress, etc. Pain and hurt from the past can cause people to become physically ill. To heal those illnesses, past things have to be confessed and worked through.

16. It is true that the Lord gives the gift of healing to some people. It does not mean, however, that only those Christians may pray for the sick. Mark 16:17-18 says; "And these signs will follow or

accompany those who believe...they will place their hands on sick people, and they will get well." Go with boldness to the Lord when praying for sick people. The time has come for James 5:13-15 to become normal practice in the church of the Lord again. "Is anyone of you in trouble? He should pray. Is anyone happy? Let him sing songs of praise. Is anyone of you sick? He should call the elders of the church to pray over him and anoint him with oil in the name of the Lord. And the prayer offered in faith will make the sick person well; the Lord will raise him up. If he has sinned, he will be forgiven."

17. When the church gathers, prayers should be offered for the sick people by name. Those who are sick should be brought to church so that they can be prayed for there. James 5 says clearly that when someone is ill, he or she must call the elders

of the church, so that they can anoint him with oil and pray for him or her.

18. God uses different "methods" to heal people:
    a) God heals through the laying on of hands;
    b) Go heals through the anointing with oil and faithful prayer;
    c) God sometimes heals people at communion;
    d) God heals people in answer to intercession for them;
    e) God uses doctors and medication to heal people.
19. Remember when you pray for someone or for yourself that healing does not always occur overnight or immediately. It can sometimes take days or weeks before someone is completely healed.
20. In Exodus 15:26 the Lord calls Himself Jahweh-Ropheka, it means: The Lord who heals you. It is

God's Name; it is whom He is, what He can do and what He wants to do. When you pray for the sick, pray to God who calls Himself Jahweh-Ropheka.

Additional Prayers

- I command every force and power, contending with the plans of God for my life this year, be expressly uprooted and destroyed in the name of Jesus.

- By the blood of the Lamb, I erase every mark of shame, disgrace and reproach against me in Jesus name.

- By the blood of Jesus I reverse and destroy every trend of disappointment, failure, poverty, shame and disgrace planted to operate in my destiny in Jesus name.

- Every power or group speaking impossibilities and failures into my life, fall down and die now in the name of Jesus.

- By fire by force, I command every satanic manipulation in my life to be overthrown and burnt by fire in the name of Jesus.

- Every satanic imagination and thoughts affecting my destiny; be expressly defeated in the name of Jesus.

- Every spiritual barrier and limitation to success and victory in my life, receive the rod of God, and be broken to irreparable pieces in the name of Jesus.

- Every ungodly experience in my life due to evil covenant, I command it to be annulled by the blood of the Lamb in the name of Jesus.

- Every force and power of the sun, moon and stars working against my destiny, I command it to be subdued to work in my favor in the name of Jesus.

- Every force and power using the earth and its elements against me, I command it to be expressly paralyzed in the name of Jesus.

- Every satanic gathering held in the air, land and sea against my destiny, be scattered by fire now in the name of Jesus.

- Every force and power, delegated to hinder and oppress my breakthrough this month, I command it to be plundered and rendered to naught in the name of Jesus.

- By the blood of the Lamb, I silence every voice speaking failure against my destiny in the name of Jesus.

- Every seed and root of near success syndrome in my life – I command it to be destroyed totally by fire in the name of Jesus.

- By the blood of Jesus, I erase all divinations and enchantments planned against me in the name of Jesus.

- By the blood of Jesus, I erase all evil handwriting against my life and destiny in the name of Jesus.

- By fire by force, I bind every evil strongman assigned to trap my blessings and destiny in the name of Jesus.

- I command every satanic scales that had been blinding my eyes from seeing the dominion God has given me – fall off by fire in the name of Jesus.

- I cancel every negative pronouncement made against my life in the name of Jesus.

- Every satanic stronghold, assigned to keep me bound in the shackles of frustration, disappointment and failure, receive the judgment of God by fire and be destroyed in the name of Jesus.

- Every force and power contending with the dreams and visions of my life that God has planned for me, what are you waiting for? I command you to fall down and die now by fire in the name of Jesus.

- Every satanic veil blocking me from seeing the plan of God for my life and destiny – I command it to be destroyed now in the name of Jesus.

- Every area of my life where failure has dominated – be restored back, in the name of Jesus.

- Every evil river flowing against my joy and peace, I command you to dry up in the name of Jesus.

- I command every satanic timing and schedules programmed against my life, be canceled in the name of Jesus.

- Every root of unfruitfulness assigned to make my life unproductive, I command you to be uprooted in the name of Jesus.

- I command all handwritings of evil, written against my destiny, to be erased by the Blood of Jesus.

- I command every evil voice speaking disaster against me in the name of Jesus.

- I command every evil strongman assigned to derail my destiny to be arrested and caged in the name of Jesus.

- I command every vision-killing agents assigned against my vision to be destroyed in the name of Jesus.

- I command every spirit that has been assigned to hinder my divine elevation to be destroyed in the name of Jesus.

- Every evil load and yoke suppressing my divine uplifting; be destroyed in the name of Jesus.

- I command every force and power released against my destiny to be arrested in the name of Jesus.

- I command every evil power contending with the purposes and plan of God for my life to be destroyed in the name of Jesus.

- I command every stronghold of family ancestral spirit working against my destiny to be destroyed in the name of Jesus.

- I command every spirit of fear operating in my life to be destroyed in the name of Jesus.

- I command every spirit of failure assigned to frustrate my progress to be destroyed in the name of Jesus.

- I command every trap of stagnation, keeping my life at the bus stop of life in the name of Jesus.

- I command every curse of rejection operating in my life to be destroyed in the name of Jesus.

- I command every spirit assigned to paralyze my future and destiny to be destroyed in the name of Jesus.

- I command every barrier limiting my progress to be destroyed in the name of Jesus.

- I command every wickedness and evil planted in the foundation of my life to be destroyed in the name of Jesus.

- I command every evil covenant entered into by myself or by anyone dead or alive to be canceled in the name of Jesus.

- I command every covering over my star to be destroyed in the name of Jesus.

- I command every form of stagnation in every area of my life to be destroyed in the name of Jesus.

- I command every mountain standing before me, blocking my advancement and progress – be moved in the name of Jesus.

- I command every spirit of manipulation designed to short-exchange my destiny – be destroyed in the name of Jesus.

- I command every dream-killer, dream-thieve assigned against my dream to be destroyed in the name of Jesus.

- I command every evil mark of failure and anti-success syndrome in my life – to be destroyed in the name of Jesus.

- I command every satanic gathering against my success and prosperity to be eternally dispersed in the name of Jesus.

- I command every spirit of death hovering over my family to be destroyed in the name of Jesus.

- I command every wall standing between my life and my breakthroughs to fall down in the name of Jesus.

- I command every evil altar where my name has been placed – to be destroyed in the name of Jesus.

- I command every cage and prison where my life has been kept and locked to bust open and be released in the name of Jesus.

- I command every evil curse and covenant working against my life to be destroyed in the name of Jesus.

- I command every works of witchcraft intended for my destruction – to be frustrated in the name of Jesus.

- I command every satanic limitations and obstacles set before me as a stumbling block to be destroyed in the name of Jesus.

- I command every evil pronouncement and incantation, spells, jinxes – pronounced against my life to be destroyed in the name of Jesus.

- I command every evil chain that is limiting my speed of progress to be destroyed in the name of Jesus.

- I command every satanic tower built to launch attacks against my life – to be destroyed in the name of Jesus.

- I command every power introducing hardships in my life to be destroyed in the name of Jesus.

- I command every obstacle in my life to be converted into opportunities in the name of Jesus.

- I command every generational curses operating in my life and the lives of my family to be broken in the name of Jesus.

Prophetic Declarations

- My ears shall hear only good news concerning my life this month.

- My life shall be a testimony of the goodness of the Lord.

- The foundations of my life are blessed.

- My star shall shine for all to see.

- My head is lifted above all my equals.

- I see all my dreams fulfilled in my lifetime.

- All my endeavors shall yield abundantly.

- I am blessed and highly favored.

- I am a carrier of grace and favor.

- My needs are divinely supplied.

- I am a winner in the race of life.

- I will enjoy the works of my hands.

- This is my season of divine upliftment and testimonies.

- The foundations of my life are blessed.

- My life is for signs and wonders.

- The grace and the peace of God is upon my life.

- I shall not be stagnant in life.

- I shall see my expected end come to pass this month.

- The anointing for greatness is upon me.

- I shall be found faithful in all that I do.

- I am the head and not the tail.

- My life shall not be barren but shall yield good and bountiful harvest.

- I shall not miss the time of my visitation.

- My time for great exploits is now!

- I shall come out of every trial triumphantly.

- I shall not be disgraced in life.

- I am divinely empowered to fly as an eagle.

- The anointing for greatness is upon my life.

- My life shall never be stagnant forever.

- I will arrive at my destination and possess my possessions.

- I am victorious in all things.

- I shall lend to nations and not borrow.

- The mercy of God shall follow me always.

- This is my month of supernatural exploits!

- I shall fulfill my destiny.

Prayer Points Against Bad Dreams

- I claim all the good things that God has revealed to me through dreams. I reject all bad and satanic dreams in the name of Jesus.

- You are going to be specific here. Place your hand on your chest and talk to God specifically about the dreams that need to be canceled. Cancel it with all your strength. If it needs fire, command the fire of God to burn it to ashes.

- Lord, perform the necessary surgical operation in my life and change all that had gone wrong in the spirit world.

- I claim back all the good things that I have lost as a result of defeat and attacks in my dreams in Jesus' name.

- I arrest every spiritual attacker and paralyze their activities in my life in the name of Jesus.

- I retrieve my stolen virtues, goodness and blessings in Jesus' name.

- Let all satanic manipulations through dreams be dissolved in Jesus' name.

- Let all arrows, gunshots, wounds, harassment, and opposition in dreams return to the sender in the name of Jesus.

- I reject every evil spiritual load placed on me through dreams in Jesus' name.

- All spiritual animals (cats, dogs, snakes, crocodiles) paraded against me should be chained and return to the senders in the name of Jesus.

- Holy Ghost, purge my intestine and my blood from satanic foods and injections.

- I break every evil covenant and initiation through dreams in the name of Jesus.

- I disband all the hosts of darkness set against me in the name of Jesus.

- Every evil imagination and plan contrary to my life should fail woefully in the name of Jesus.

- Every doorway and ladder to satanic invasion in my life should be abolished forever by the Blood of Jesus.

- I loose myself from curses, hexes, spells, bewitchment and evil domination directed against me through dreams in the name of Jesus.

- I command you ungodly powers, release me in the name of Jesus.

- Let all past satanic defeats in the dream be converted to victory in the name of Jesus.

- Let all the test in the dream be converted to testimonies in Jesus' name.

- Let all trials in the dream be converted to triumphs in Jesus' name.

- Let all failures in the dream be converted to success in Jesus' name.

- Let all scars in the dream be converted to stars in Jesus' name.

- Let all bondage in the dream be converted to freedom in Jesus' name.

- Let all losses in the dream be converted to gains in Jesus' name.

- Let all opposition in the dream be converted to victory in Jesus' name.

- Let all weaknesses in the dream be converted to strength in Jesus' name.

- Let all negative in the dream be converted to positive in Jesus' name.

- I release myself from every infirmity introduced into my life through dreams in the name of Jesus.

- Let all attempts by the enemy to deceive me through dreams fail woefully in the name of Jesus.

- I reject evil spiritual husband, wife, children, marriage, engagement, trading, pursuit, ornament, money, friend, relative, etc. in the name of Jesus.

- Lord Jesus, wash my spiritual eyes ears and mouth with your blood.

- The God who answers by fire should answer by fire whenever any spiritual attacker against me.

- Lord Jesus, replace all satanic dreams with heavenly visions and divinely -inspired dreams.

- Let the blood of Jesus wash all the organs in my body in the name of Jesus.

- Confess these scriptures out loud: (Psalm 27: 1-2, 1 Cor. 10:21, Psalm 91)

- I command every evil plantation in my life, COME OUT WITH ALL YOUR ROOTS in the name of Jesus! (Lay your hands on your stomach and keep repeating the emphasized area.)

- Evil strangers in my body, come all the way out of your hiding places in the name of Jesus.

- I disconnect any conscious or unconscious linkage with demonic caterers in the name of Jesus.

- Let all avenues of eating or drinking spiritual poisons be close in the name of Jesus.

- I cough out and vomit any food eaten from the table of the devil in the name of Jesus. (Cough them out and vomit them in faith. Prime the expulsion).

- Let all negative materials circulating in my blood stream be evacuated in the name of Jesus.

- Let all evil spiritual feeders warring against me drink their own blood and eat their own flesh.

- I command all demonic food utensils fashioned against me to be roasted in the name of Jesus.

- Holy Ghost fire, circulate all over my body.

- I command all physical poisons inside my system to be neutralized in the name of Jesus.

- Let all evil assignments fashioned against me through the mouth gate be nullified in the name of Jesus.

- Let all spiritual problems attached to any hour of the night be canceled in the name of Jesus. (Pick the periods from 12 midnight down to 6:00 am)

- Bread of heaven, fill me till I want no more.

- Let all catering equipment of evil caterers attached to me be destroyed in the name of Jesus.

- I command my digestive system to reject every evil command in the name of Jesus.

- Let all satanic designs of oppression against me in dreams and visions be frustrated in the name of Jesus.

- I remove my name from the register of evil feeders with the blood of Jesus.

- Let the habitation of evil caterers become desolate in the name of Jesus.

BIBLE VERSES

- I paralyze the spirit that brings bad dreams to me in the name of Jesus.

- Let the fire of the Holy Ghost destroy any evil list containing my name of Jesus.

- Let the fire of the Holy Ghost destroy any evil list containing my name in the name of Jesus.

- I destroy any coffin prepared for me in the name of Jesus.

- I cancel and wipe off all evil dreams in the name of Jesus.

- I destroy every satanic accident organized for my sake in the name of Jesus.

- I render all evil night creatures powerless in the name of Jesus.

- Let the blood of Jesus wash all the organs in my body in the name of Jesus.

- Let all sicknesses planted in my life through evil spiritual food be destroyed in the name of Jesus.

- Let the blood of Jesus erase all evil dreams in the name of Jesus.

- Let the fire of God boil all rivers harboring unfriendly demons in the name of Jesus.

- Let all evil dreams be replaced with blessings in the name of Jesus.

- I command all my good dreams to come to pass in the name of Jesus.

- Father, hasten the performance of my good dreams.

Printed in Dunstable, United Kingdom